1-2-3 DRAW CARTOON TRUCKS AND MOTORCYCLES

A Step-by-Step Guide

by Steve Barr

*To Danny, Kris, and Aaron—
My great, fun friends who have
spent many days hiking in the
mountains with me. We've seen
great sights and no matter what
we've encountered along the way
the Gholdston crew just kept on
"truckin"!*

Printed in China

Library of Congress Cataloging-in-Publication Data

Barr, Steve, 1958-
    1-2-3 draw cartoon trucks and motorcycles : a step-by-step guide / by
Steve Barr.
        p. cm. --   (1-2-3 draw)
    Includes bibliographical references and index.
    ISBN 0-939217-77-5 (alk. paper)
    1.   Motor vehicles in art--Juvenile literature. 2.   Cartooning--Technique--
Juvenile literature.   I. Title: Cartoon trucks and motorcycles. II. Title: One-two-
three draw cartoon trucks and motorcycles. III. Title.
    NC1764.8.M67B37 2005
    741.5--dc22
                                        2004027141

Distributed to the trade and art
markets in North America by

NORTH LIGHT BOOKS,
an imprint of F&W Publications, Inc.
4700 East Galbraith Road
Cincinnati, OH 45236

(800) 289-0963

Table of Contents

Stop! Look! Listen!

Before You Begin

You will need:

1   a sharpened pencil

2   paper

3   an eraser

4   a pencil sharpener

5   colored pencils, markers, or crayons

6   a comfortable place to sit and draw

7   a good light source so you can see what you're doing!

Note

If you have trouble drawing perfect circles or straight lines by hand, it is fine to use a ruler or trace around something circular while you are using this book. Just remember, there are NO RULES in cartooning....so it's okay if your shapes and lines aren't perfect!

Ready! Set! Let's draw!

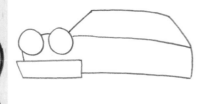
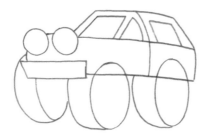
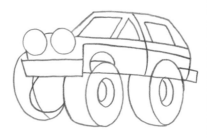

NO RULES!

There are no rules in cartooning! You can do whatever you want with your drawings! Inanimate objects can come to life! Your drawings don't have to look like real trucks or real motorcycles. You can change anything about them that you want. You can give them huge tires or tiny tires. You can turn headlights into eyes. Windshields can become faces. They are cartoons, and cartooning has NO RULES!

Sketch, doodle, and play!

The more you practice, the better you will become. Sketch, doodle, and play with your drawings. Cartooning is about having a great time. If you don't like the way a drawing looks in this book, change it! The more you change, the better. Make each drawing uniquely yours.

A few cartooning tips

1 Draw lightly at first—SKETCH gently so you can erase extra lines in your final drawing.

2 Practice, practice, practice! I've been doing this for years, and I still practice in my spare time.

3 Have FUN drawing cartoons! If you think you messed up, just erase that part and change your art to make it better.

Basic Shapes and Lines

Here are samples of the various lines and shapes you will use in this book.

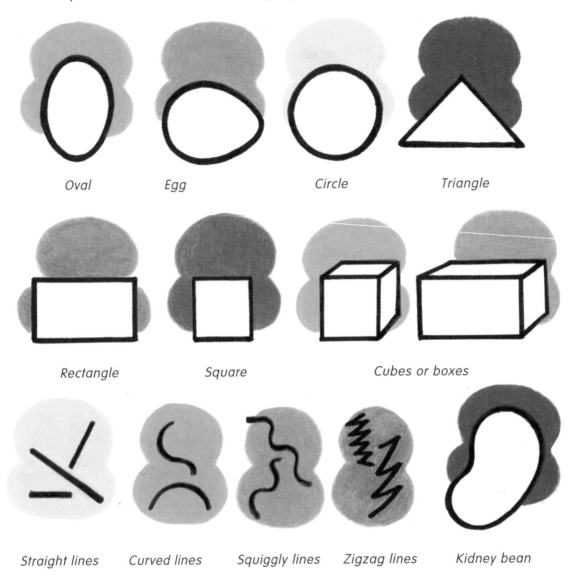

Oval	*Egg*	*Circle*	*Triangle*

Rectangle	*Square*	*Cubes or boxes*

Straight lines	*Curved lines*	*Squiggly lines*	*Zigzag lines*	*Kidney bean*

Note: If you have trouble sketching a perfect circle or a straight line by hand, it is fine to trace something round or to use a ruler. Professional cartoonists use tools to help them get their drawings just right. Remember that cartooning has NO RULES. It is fine if your circles and straight lines are a little shaky.

How Professional Cartoonists Work

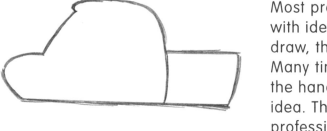

Most professional cartoonists start with ideas of what they want to draw, then try to put them on paper. Many times it doesn't come out of the hand exactly like the original idea. That's okay, because a professional cartoonist can change and correct things as he goes along.

I start by doodling basic shapes lightly on a clean sheet of paper. As the drawing begins to look the way I want it to, I gently erase any extra sketch lines. Once I get the rough drawing just right, I trace the remaining lines with a bold pen. Any little "glitches" or adjustments that need to be done are taken care of in the final inking stage. Once the inked drawing is finished, color is added.

To use this book, you do not need a pen to do your final art. You can just darken the final lines with pencil. Practicing with pencil drawings is a great way to begin to learn. Once your pencil sketches get really good, you might want to try experimenting with a pen to make your cartoons even better.

STEVE BARR

Expressions (Side View)

You can turn anything into a cartoon character just by giving it a face! Adding faces to windshields, headlights, or body parts transforms them into cartoons and can bring trucks or motorcycles to life. The keys to drawing facial expressions are the mouth and eyes. Using simple lines and shapes, you can make great expressions.

Practice drawing some of the side views of the expressions you see below. You can then, create new ones of your own. Experiment with different ones on each of the vehicles you draw from this book.

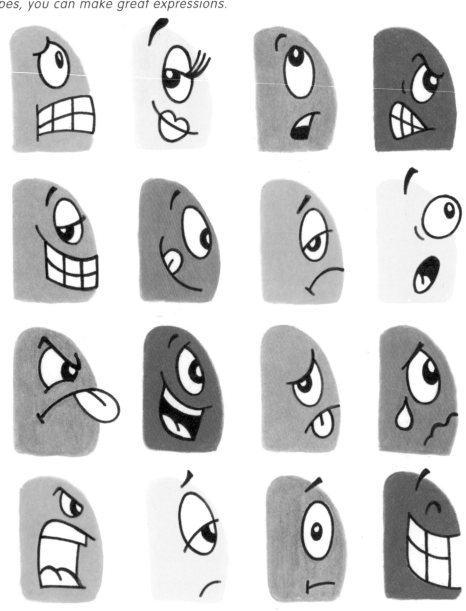

Expressions (Front View)

On many of the trucks and motorcycles in this book you will want to draw an expression from a front view. Practice drawing some of these expressions. As you go through the lessons in this book, use some of them on your drawings.

Tip: Look in a mirror and make a face at yourself. Pay attention to the lines your mouth, eyes, and eyebrows make. Try to mimic them on paper using simple shapes and lines.

Motion

Using simple lines and shapes, you can show action in your cartoons. Let's draw a pickup truck and make it look like it's moving.

1 Lightly sketch a long rectangle for the body. Sketch a square on top of the rectangle for the cab.

2 Look closely at the shapes emerging. Using straight lines, draw the windshield and wheel wells.

3 Using curved lines, draw the roof and the front of the hood.

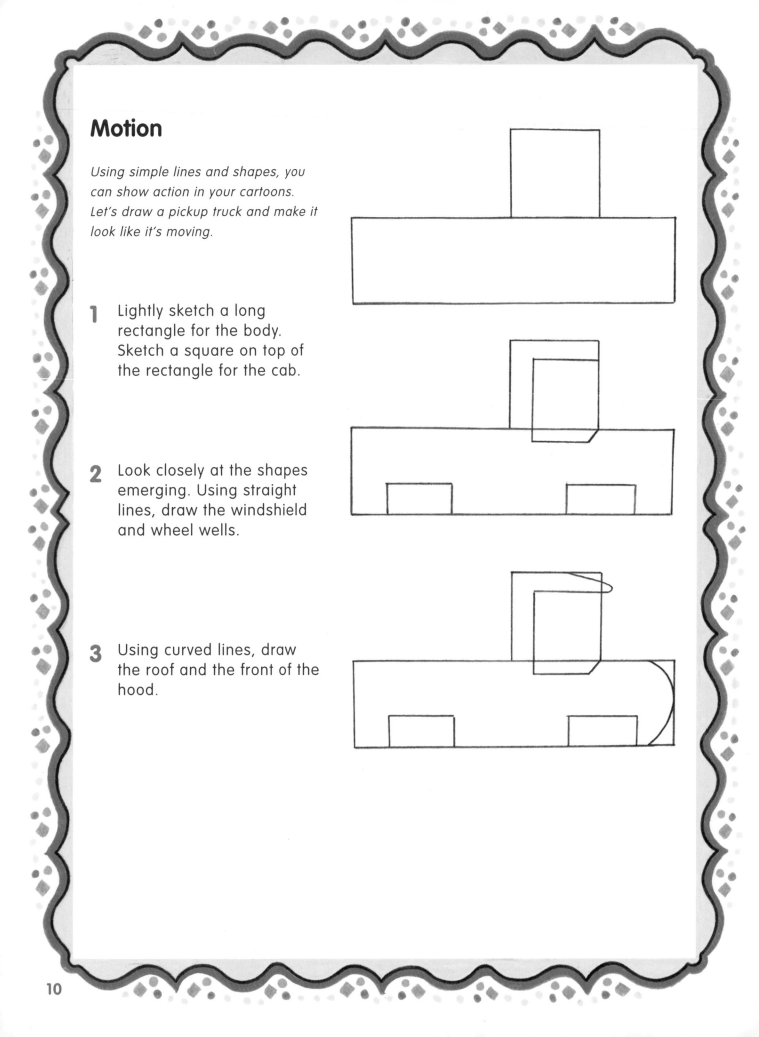

4 Draw a rectangle for the rear bumper. Add curved lines for a headlight.

5 Look closely! Add the happy face. Draw tilted ovals for tires. If you tilt them toward the front of the truck, it makes it look like the pickup is flying down the road. Add a few curved and straight lines to make it look like it is really moving. Erase extra sketch lines. Darken the lines. Add color.

6 If you tilt the wheels in the other direction, it looks like your truck is skidding to a stop. Add squiggly lines to make skid marks under the tires and curved lines in front of the truck to make it look like it is shaking. Change the expression to make your truck look startled.

Add words near the truck to show the sound it would make.

Antique Truck

Antique trucks have a very square look to them. Let's use a different technique to draw an old pickup.

1 Lightly sketch a straight line to use as a guide for tires. Draw two circles for wheels.

2 Look closely! Draw long straight lines for the bottom of the truck. Add curved lines to the front for a wheel well. Draw two circles in the center of each wheel.

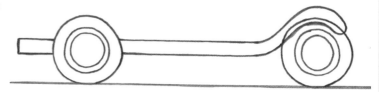

3 Look at the body shape. Using straight lines, draw the body. Add small circles in the center of each tire. Draw straight lines for spokes.

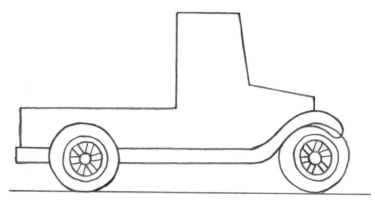

4 Using curved lines, shape the roof. Add a straight line and a curved end to the back of the truck. Using straight lines, draw the door and the hood.

5 Look at the structure on the back of the truck. Using straight lines, add it. Look at the shapes on the front of the truck. Draw the radiator cap and the headlight.

6 Look at the final drawing! Erase extra sketch lines. Darken the final lines. Add a face inside the windshield, then color your cartoon.

Tanker

Tanker trucks have huge cylinders on the back to carry liquid like milk or fuel. Let's draw a cartoon tanker!

1 Look at the tanker (hot dog) shape. Using curved lines, lightly sketch it.

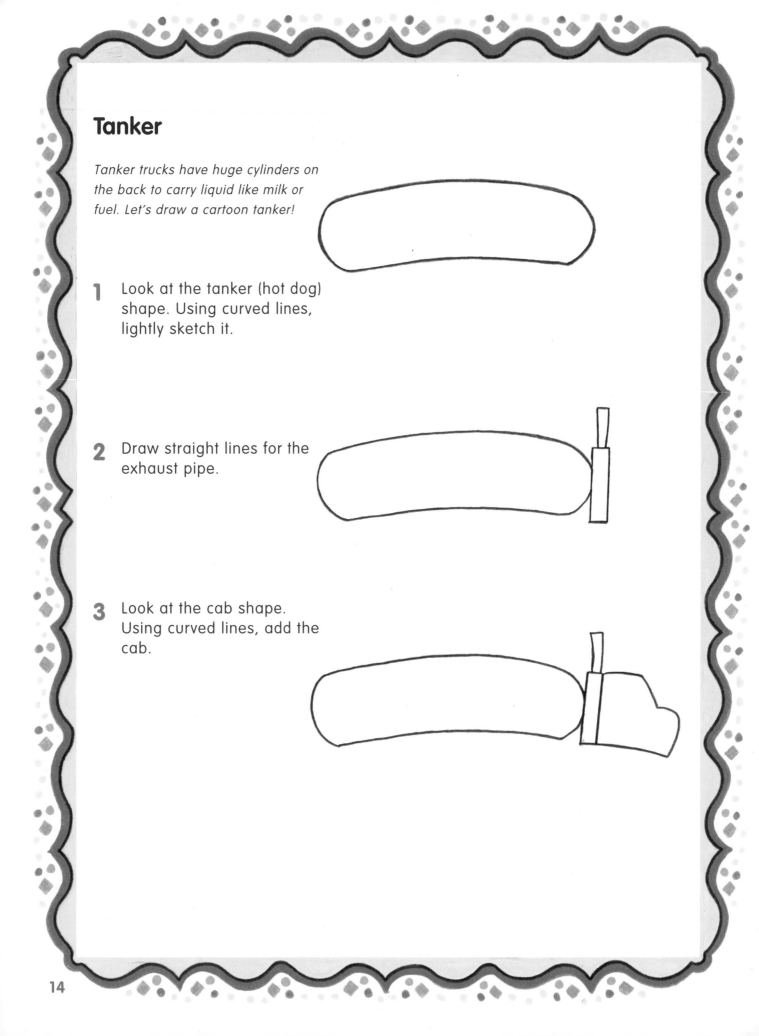

2 Draw straight lines for the exhaust pipe.

3 Look at the cab shape. Using curved lines, add the cab.

4 Look closely! Draw the triangle shape on top of the cab. Using curved lines, add two cap shapes on top of the tanker. Draw a curved line along the side of the tank.

5 Look at the six wheels and their positions. Using tilted ovals draw the wheels. Add windows and a front bumper.

6 Look closely! Erase extra lines. Darken the final lines. Add a face on the cab. Add color.

Tip: Curved lines around the truck and tires show movement. Leaving a little space between the wheels and the ground makes it look like your tanker is flying!

Tow Truck

Since cartoon trucks don't have to look realistic, let's make a tow truck that is really silly looking.

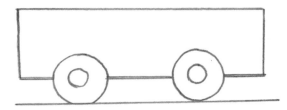

1 Look closely! Lightly sketch a straight guide line for the ground. Draw a circle inside a circle for each tire. Using straight lines, draw the rectangle-shaped body.

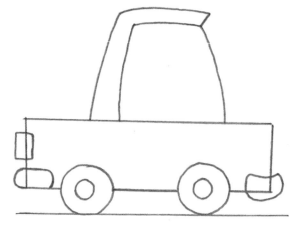

2 Look at the shape of the top. Using long curved lines, draw the cab. Look at the taillight and bumpers. Add these.

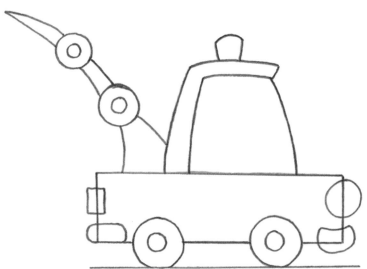

3 Look at the shapes that begin the towing equipment. Draw these. Add a curved light on top of the roof.

4 Look at the lines and the shapes on the tow line. Draw these. Sketch an oval and two straight lines inside the window for a driver.

5 Draw an eyebrow, eye, big nose, mouth, and lines to begin a moustache. Add an ear and a hair line. Draw a hat for the driver.

6 Look at the final drawing! Erase extra lines. Darken the remaining lines. Add the details you see and color.

Terrific!

Car Carrier

Car carriers carry cars from the factory to dealerships. Let's draw a cartoon car carrier! (That's a mouthful, isn't it?)

1 Lightly sketch the ground line. Look closely at the spaces between the tires. Draw the tires and a circle in the center of each. Look at the shape of the cab and the bed of the carrier. Draw the body.

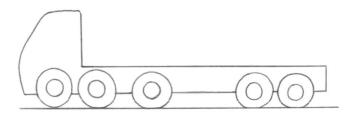

2 Look at the lines that shape the back of the carrier. Using straight and curved lines draw it.

3 Look at the exhaust pipe system between the cab and the back. Draw it.

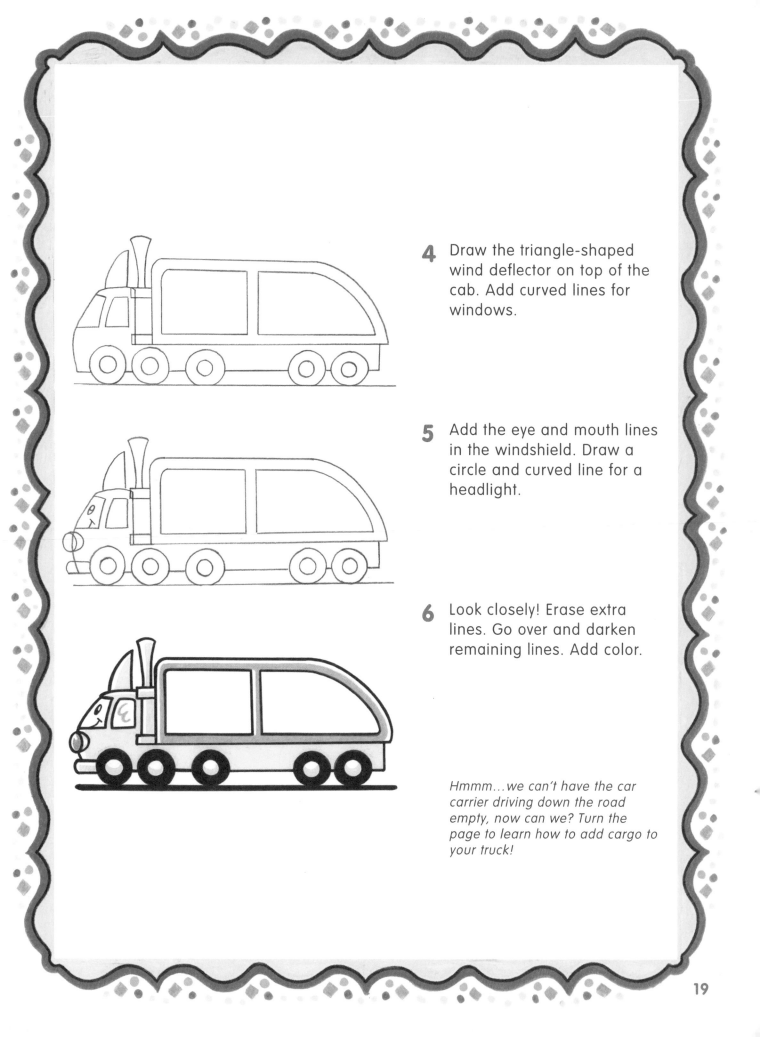

4 Draw the triangle-shaped wind deflector on top of the cab. Add curved lines for windows.

5 Add the eye and mouth lines in the windshield. Draw a circle and curved line for a headlight.

6 Look closely! Erase extra lines. Go over and darken remaining lines. Add color.

Hmmm…we can't have the car carrier driving down the road empty, now can we? Turn the page to learn how to add cargo to your truck!

Cargo

Do you think they call it cargo because this is how the car goes to the dealer? Let's add some minivans to the back of the car carrier.

1   Look closely. Draw tires on the top of the truck for the first minivan.

2   Next add a straight line for the bottom of the van. Draw a long curved line to finish the body.

3   Draw curved lines for windows.

4 Add an oval for a headlight. Draw the curved bumpers. Add a taillight.

5 If you'd like, you can add a face to the minivan's windshield. Erase extra lines.

6 Draw three more minivans to give your car carrier a full load! Darken final lines. Add color.

Great job!

Cement Truck

Let's draw a cartoon cement truck! They're a "barrel of fun"!

1 Sketch a straight line for the ground. Draw circles for wheels. Add a straight line for the bottom of the body.

2 Look at the front bumper. Using straight lines, draw it. Look at the cab shape. Draw the cab. Add a curved line over the front wheel for a wheel well. Look at the back shape. Draw the lines you see.

3 Look at the four shapes that form the exhaust pipe. Add these. Look at the lines that shape the gas tank between the wheels. Draw these. Look at the back of the truck. Add the lines you see.

4 Starting at the front, add a curved line for a headlight. Use long curved lines to add the cement mixer.

5 Draw a face in the windshield. Look at the tires and wheels. Add tiny circles in the center of each tire for lug nuts. Draw small triangles along the edges of each tire for treads.

6 Look at the final drawing. Erase extra sketch lines. Darken the final lines. Add color.

Delivery Truck

Small trucks run all over the place delivering things to businesses. Let's draw a funny cartoon delivery truck.

1 Look closely at the outline of the truck. Using curved and straight lines, sketch it. Look at the oval shaped tires. Draw the tires.

2 Look at the shape of the cab. Using straight lines, draw it. Add curved lines for the windshield and headlight. Draw a small rectangle for the rear bumper.

3 Look at the wild shape of the driver's head. Looks fish-like! Using curved lines, draw it. Add a steering wheel.

4 Look at the driver again. Using curved lines, add the dorsal fin, an eyebrow, and front fins.

5 Draw straight lines to divide the dorsal fin. Add curved lines for the eyes and mouth.

6 Look closely! Erase extra lines. Darken the remaining lines. Add color.

FRESH FISH

You can write anything you want on the side of your truck. Have fun and make up something silly. The police are bound to pull over this "fishy" looking truck.

Garbage Truck

Another method used to draw trucks is freehand. That means freely sketching (doodling) shapes to create what you want to draw. Let's draw a garbage truck!

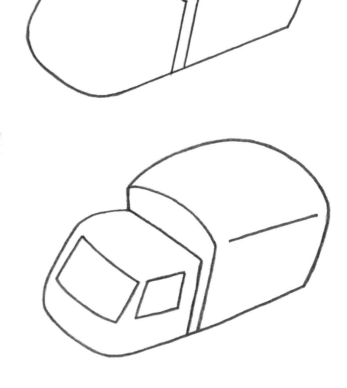

1 Look closely at the shapes and lines that begin this truck. Freely sketch the curved and straight lines you see.

2 Draw curved lines for windows. Add a straight line to the side of the truck.

3 Using curved lines, draw lights on the roof and on the back. Add round headlights.

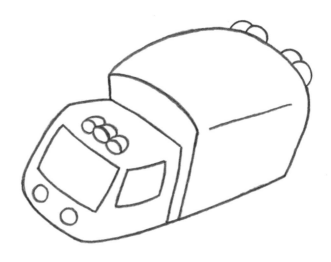

4 Draw ovals for tires.

5 Look at that happy face. Draw it.

6 Look at the final drawing. Erase extra lines. Darken the final lines. Add color.

Happy truck in spite of having a job that stinks!

Rental Truck

Many people rent trucks when they are moving to new homes. Let's draw a cool cartoon rental truck!

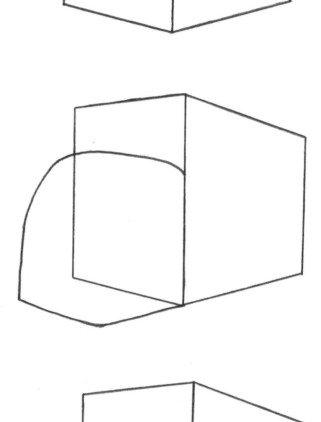

1 Look at the shape of this cube. Using straight lines, lightly sketch it

2 Look at the shape of the cab emerging. Using curved and straight lines, add it.

3 Add curved lines for windows. Look at the shape of the front bumper. Draw it.

4 Draw the rectangular headlights. Add a running light under the driver's window. Add curved lines to the right front and bottom left edges of the trailer.

5 Draw a smiling face inside the windshield. Draw ovals for tires.

6 Look closely! Erase extra lines. Darken the final lines. Add color. Make up a funny name for the rental company and write it on the side of your truck.

Good job! That's a drawing that really moves me....

U-HALT

Commercial Truck

Medium sized trucks are used for commercial deliveries by lots of companies. You can add even more character to your truck by adding more details. Let's draw a wacky looking commercial truck.

1 Look at the beginning shapes of this truck. Sketch curved lines to shape the cab. Add straight lines to form a cube for the back.

2 Draw circles and curved lines on the cab for eyeglasses.

3 Look at the lines that form the windows. Add these. Put a curved line above the side window. Draw the eyes. Add a curved line for the mouth.

4 Look closely! Using curved lines, draw the arms, hands, and thumbs. Add the rectangular headlights.

5 Draw curved lines on each hand for fingers. Add ovals and curved lines for tires.

6 Look at the final drawing. Erase extra lines. Darken the final lines. Add color.

Now, that's a truck that likes to make a spectacle of itself!

Fire Truck

Fire trucks race to help in emergencies when there is a fire. Let's draw an old-fashioned fire truck with a brave firefighter inside!

1 Look closely at the beginning wheels and the rectangles between them . Sketch ovals for wheels. Connect them with straight lines.

2 Look at the shape of the emerging body. Using straight lines, draw the outline of the body.

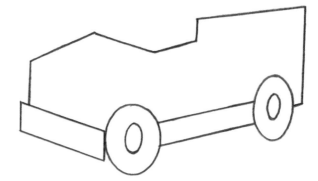

3 Look again! Starting at the top, draw the ladder. Add the windshield. Using ovals and curved lines, draw the lights. Draw straight lines and curved lines to add a ladder. Add the rear bumper.

4 Starting at the top, draw the head, hat, and nose. Add two straight lines for the shoulders. Draw the grill and radiator lines.

5 Add the curved lines on the top of the hat. Add ovals for eyes. Draw curved lines for hair, ears, and a smile.

6 Look closely! Erase extra lines. Darken the final lines. Add color.

Now that's one truck that's fired up and ready to go!

Exaggeration

One of the essential elements of cartooning is exaggeration. Let's draw a oversized driver in a really small vehicle.

1 Let's begin by drawing the oversized driver. Sketch the oval head, ears, and eyes.

2 Look at the shape of the hat. Draw curved lines and a small circle for the hat. Using curved lines, add the eyebrows, eyes, and mouth. Draw curved lines for a skinny neck.

3 Starting at the top, add a puff of curly hair above his ear. Draw a rectangle for the windshield at the base of the neck. Add straight lines for shoulders. Leave room to add arms.

4 Look again! Draw straight lines for a sleeve and arm. Draw curved lines to shape a hand and the steering wheel. Add additional straight lines to begin the cab and hood of the truck.

5 Look at the shape of the truck emerging. Using straight lines, draw the cab front and long trailer.

6 Look at the added details. Using curved lines, draw a side window, wheel wells, and tires. Draw rectangles for headlights. Add the curved front bumper.

7 Look at the final drawing. Erase extra lines. Darken the final lines. Add color.

Great job!

Road Rage

Sometimes in traffic, drivers lose their tempers. Traffic jams, construction, and other problems make them really angry. Let's draw a really grumpy looking tractor trailer. We'll draw a front view and start at the bottom.

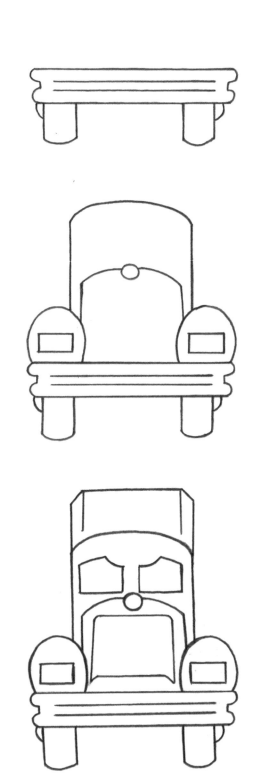

1 Look closely at the front bumper, tires, and hub caps. Using straight and curved lines, draw the bumper. Add the tires and hub caps.

2 Look at the emerging cab shapes. Draw a half oval for wheel wells on each side. Add triangles for headlights. Using straight and curved lines, draw the hood and cab. Add a small oval in the center of the hood.

3 Look at the grill shape. Draw it. Look at the shape of the front windshields. Using straight and curved lines, add the windshields. Draw straight lines to add the trailer top.

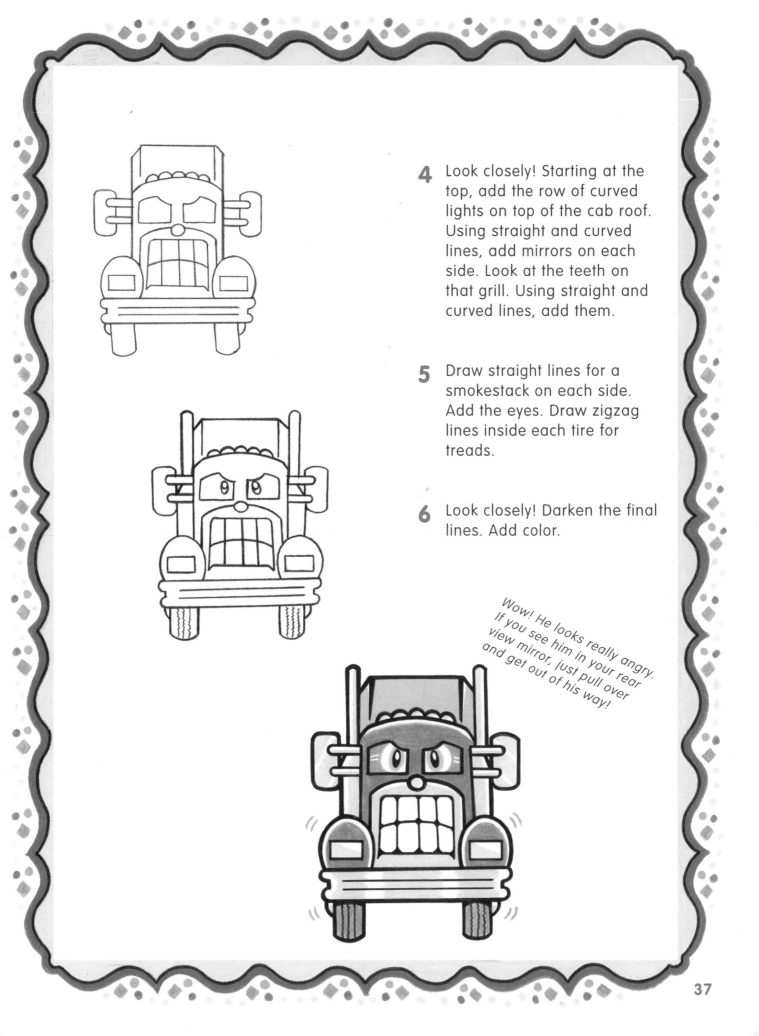

4 Look closely! Starting at the top, add the row of curved lights on top of the cab roof. Using straight and curved lines, add mirrors on each side. Look at the teeth on that grill. Using straight and curved lines, add them.

5 Draw straight lines for a smokestack on each side. Add the eyes. Draw zigzag lines inside each tire for treads.

6 Look closely! Darken the final lines. Add color.

Wow! He looks really angry. If you see him in your rear view mirror, just pull over and get out of his way!

Tractor trailer

Most tractor trailer drivers are safe drivers and friendly people. Let's draw a happy tractor trailer.

1 Look at the shapes that form this cab and front bumper. Using curved lines, sketch them.

2 Starting at the top, add curved lines on the roof for lights. Look at the curved windows. Add the windows. Draw ovals and curved lines for the wheels and the gas tank.

3 Draw long curved lines for the exhaust pipe and a wind deflector. Add small rectangles for headlights.

4 Look at the angle of the trailer. Using straight lines, sketch the trailer. Draw small ovals in the tires to add hubcaps.

5 Look again! What additional details do you see? Add these.

6 Look at the final drawing. Erase extra sketch lines. Darken the final lines. Add color.

Keep on truckin'!

Camper

Campers are great little trucks. Some even have portable kitchens and bathrooms inside them. They are great for little getaways. Let's draw a cartoon camper!

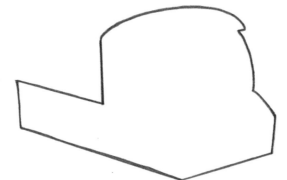

1   Look at the beginning shape. Using straight and curved lines, sketch it.

2   Draw curved lines for windows. Add curved lines and ovals for tires.

3   Look at the shape that forms the camper. Using curved lines, draw it. Look at the grill. Using straight lines, draw the rectangle shaped grill.

4 Using curved lines add windows to the camper. Draw small ovals in the grill for headlights. Add a short curved line on the left side of the hood.

5 Draw straight lines on the side of the camper for decorative stripes. Add a smiling face inside the windshield. Draw straight lines between the headlights.

6 Look closely! Erase extra sketch lines. Darken the remaining lines. Add color.

Happy Camper!

Dump Truck

Dump trucks are powerful machines that can carry huge loads of gravel, sand, and other things to construction sites. Let's create a cartoon dump truck at an angle!

1   Starting at the bottom, draw a rectangle for a bumper. Using straight lines, add the grill and radiator cap.

2   Look at the shapes of the wheel wells. Draw the right wheel well. Draw the straight lines that form the left wheel well. Using curved lines and an oval, add the front wheels.

3   Look at the shape of the cab and windows. Using straight lines, draw them. Look at the shape of the gas tank and rear wheel well. Using curved lines, add these.

4 Starting at the top, draw rectangles and curved lines for the exhaust pipe. Add long curved lines to create the front and side of the dumper. Draw ovals and curved lines for the rear tires.

5 Look at the shape of the back of the dumper. Using straight lines, draw it. Use little curved lines to add a load of sand in the back. Draw the happy face.

6 Look at the final drawing. Erase extra lines. Darken the final lines. Add color.

Looks like it leads a constructive life! Great cartooning!

Monster Truck

Monster trucks have huge tires and incredible suspension systems. At shows, they drive over the tops of cars and crush them. Let's draw a cool monster truck!

1 Look at the lines forming the beginning body shape and bumper. Sketch the lines you see.

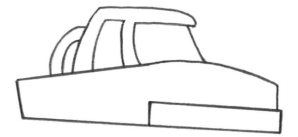

2 Look closely! Using curved lines, add the cab, windows, and a roll-bar.

3 Look at those monster wheels. Using curved lines and ovals, draw the wheels and the front axle. Add a rectangle for the grill.

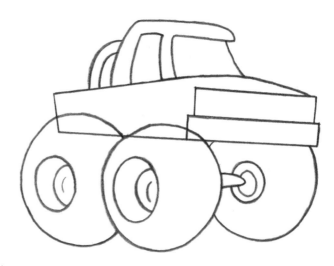

4 Look at the headlights. Add these. Using curved lines, draw a wheel well and suspension. Add curved lines to the tires.

5 Draw a face on the windshield. Add curved lines on the side of the truck. Draw short curved lines on the tires for treads.

6 Look closely! Erase extra lines. Darken the remaining lines. Add color.

To make it look like dirt is flying around your monster truck's wheels, add curved lines and small circles. Draw curved lines behind the truck for smoke.

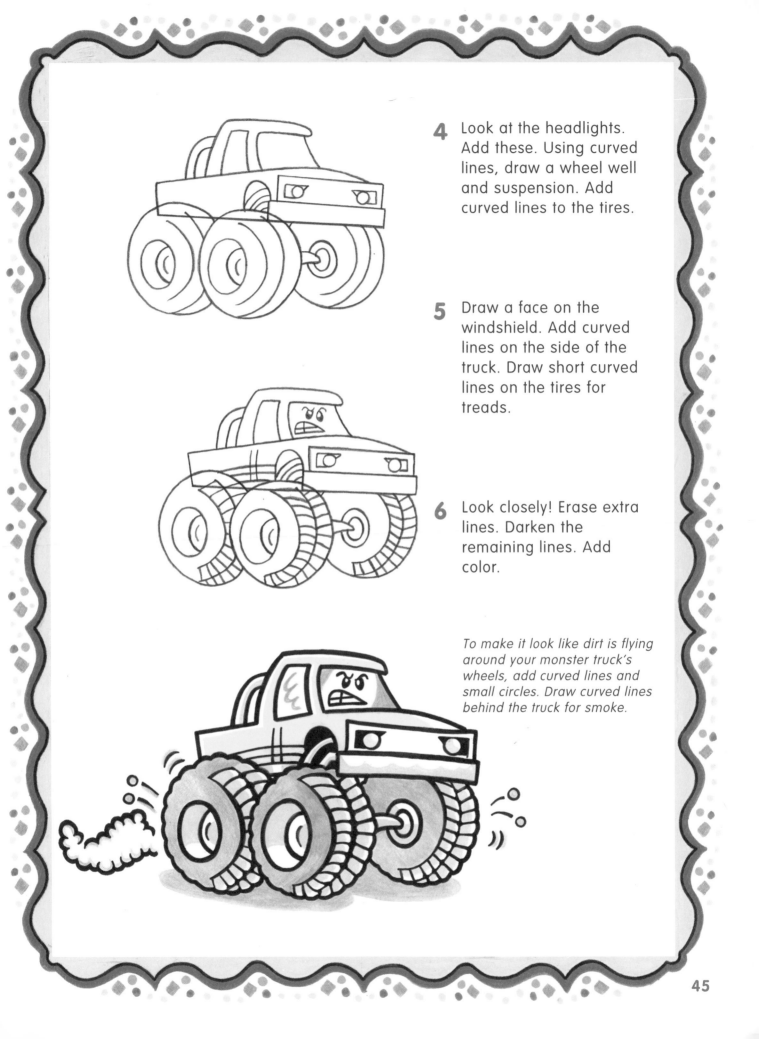

Motorcycle (Rear View)

It's really easy to draw a rear view of a motorcycle. Let's draw one using very simple shapes, then learn a neat trick at the end.

1   Sketch a circle for the helmet. Add two straight lines in the center of the helmet.

2   Sketch curved lines for the rider's shoulders and torso. Add a circle for a taillight.

3   Using curved lines, add the arms. Look at the shape of the rider's legs and the back of the motorcycle. Draw the lines you see.

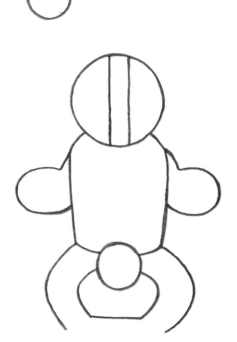

4 Look closely! Add the handlebars. Draw the rear tire and oval shaped feet.

5 Look at the final drawing on the left. Erase extra lines. Darken the final lines. Add color.

6 Look at the drawing on the right. Tilt your paper to the right as you draw the cyclist and motorcycle again. When you straighten the paper, it will look the motorcycle is leaning to make a turn!

Motorcycle (Side View)

You can begin drawing great motorcycles by using basic shapes as anchor points, then building the rest of the drawing around them.

1   Lightly sketch an oval for a gas tank. Draw a seat next to it.

2   Look at the round wheels. Draw them. Look at the lines that begin the suspension fork of the motorcycle. Add the lines you see.

3   Look closely! Using curved lines, add the handlebars. Look at the shape of the head light and the suspension bar. Using curved lines, draw these.

4   Starting at the front, add curved lines for the front wheel guard. Draw the curved exhaust pipe. Add the straight bars under the seat.

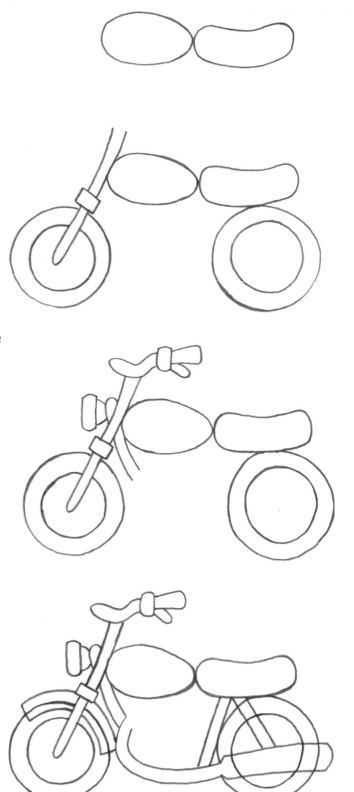

5 Look at the engine parts. Add these and two straight lines under them.

6 Draw a fun face on the gas tank. Add little lines and circles to complete the engine. Draw curved lines for a light and wheel guard in the back.

7 Look closely! Erase extra lines. Darken the remaining lines. Add color.

Chopper

Choppers have front wheel suspensions that extend way out in front of the bikes, with tiny wheels on the ends. Let's draw a mean chopper!

1   Sketch an oval for the gas tank and a curved seat next to it. Look at how they are positioned.

2   Look at the curved lines that begin the bike frame. Draw these lines and add the round headlight.

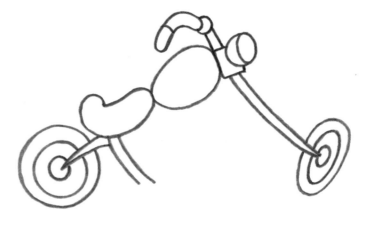

3   Look closely! Starting at the top, draw the curved handlebar. Add ovals for the front wheel. Draw circles for the rear wheel.

4 Add an oval below the gas tank. Draw curved lines for the exhaust pipe.

5 Look at the engine details. Add these.

6 Look at the final drawing. Erase extra lines. Add a mean face to the gas tank. Darken the final lines. Add color.

Draw squiggly lines around the tires to make flames shooting out of your chopper!

Touring Bike

Touring bikes are built for comfort on long trips. Let's use a technique called "blocking out" to start this bike. First you draw an anchor point, then sketch around it to create the shapes you want.

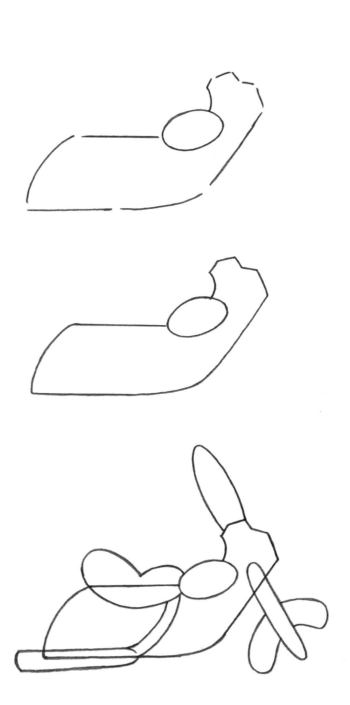

1 Our anchor point will be the oval shaped gas tank. Sketch it. Look at the basic outline. Sketch little disconnected lines to form the shape of the body. Sketch, erase, and rework your sketch until you get it just right!

2 Once you have the body shaped the way you want it, go over and connect the sketch lines.

3 Look at the top of the bike. Draw the curved shaped windshield. Using curved lines, add the front fork and the wheel guard. Draw a kidney bean shaped seat. Add the long exhaust pipe.

4 Draw curved lines for additional pipes. Using curved lines and circles, add the tires.

5 Starting at the front, add the curved handlebar and brake control. Using straight lines, draw the headlight. Draw a small curved line and two circles under the gas tank. Add a cooler behind the seat.

6 Look closely! Erase extra lines. Darken the final lines. Add color and details.

Great touring bike!

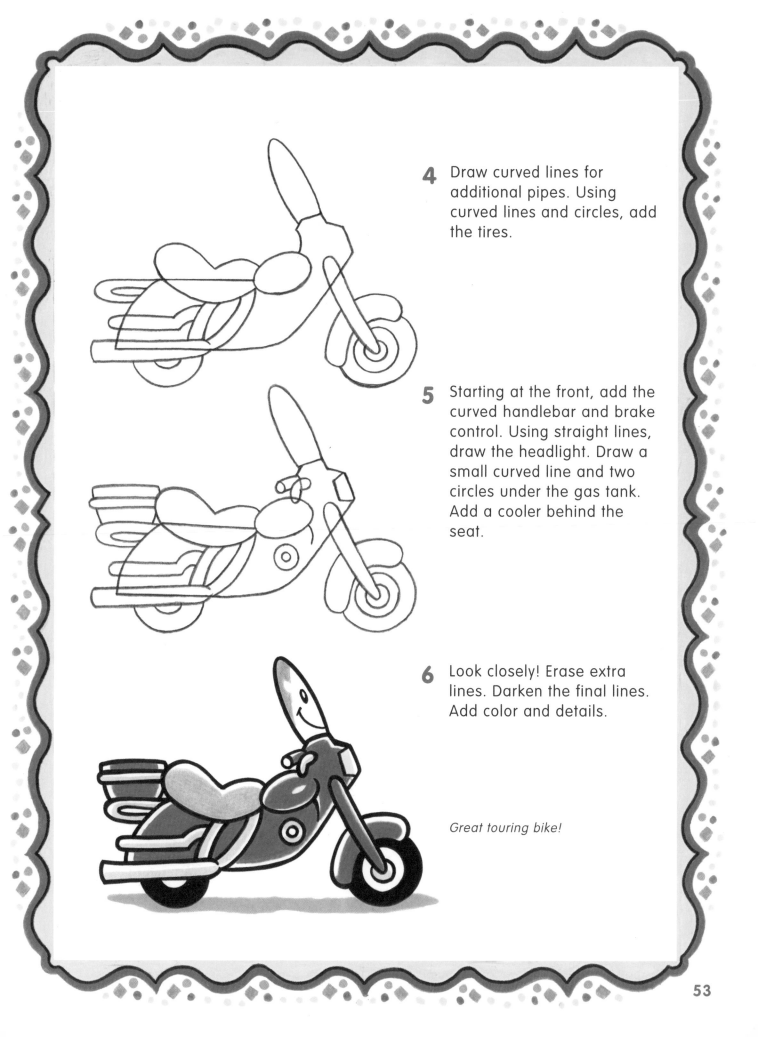

Lady Biker

It's lots of fun drawing people on your cartoon bikes. Let's draw a lady biker!

1 Look at the shapes that form her head and upper body. Sketch a squashed oval for her head. Draw a curved line for the helmet. Add short straight lines for her neck. Using curved lines, sketch her upper body.

2 Look at the sitting position of her lower body, leg, and foot. Using curved lines, draw her skirt, leg and boot. Look at the position of the rear wheel. Draw it.

3 Look closely! Using curved lines, draw her arm, hand, handlebar, and front fork. Add the round gas tank and a curved line under her leg for the seat. Draw the rear wheel guard. Add a curved line to the rear tire.

4 Starting at the front, draw the headlight and the front fork. Add ovals for the front tire. Draw the curved exhaust pipe. Add the rear wheel well. Look at the back rest and support bar. Draw the lines you see.

5 Add long curved lines for flowing hair, or design a hairdo of your own! Draw her face. Add engine details.

6 Look at the final drawing. Erase extra lines. Darken the remaining lines. Add color.

She's having a blast!

Guy Biker

Let's draw a guy riding a motorcycle.

1   Look at the shapes and lines that begin this biker. Starting at the top, sketch the lines you see.

2   Look at his face. Draw it. Using curved lines, add his hand and the handlebar grips. Draw an oval for his shoe.

3   Look at the shapes and lines of the motorcycle. Starting at the front, draw the wheel, tire, and tire guard. Add the long curved front fork. Using curved lines, draw the gas tank and a seat. Add the back wheel, tire, and tire guard.

4   Starting at the front, add the headlight, the support and suspension bars, and the exhaust pipe. Add two straight lines running from the seat to the center of the rear tire.

5 Look closely! Add additional details you see.

6 Look at the final drawing. Erase extra lines. Darken the final lines. Add color.

Tip: Tilt your drawing paper to the left when you are drawing the bike on the bottom. When you straighten the paper out your biker will be "popping a wheelie"!

You can turn your biker guy into a biker gal by adding eyelashes, long hair, and a skirt.

Sidecar

Sidecars are great! (They are the perfect place for a passenger to relax while cruising around with a biker.) Let's draw a cartoon sidecar.

1 Look at the beginning shape. Starting with the sidecar, sketch the lines and shapes you see.

2 Look closely! Using curved lines, draw the passenger's helmet and shoulders. Look at the shapes and lines that begin the motorcycle. Using curved lines, draw these. Draw a headlight and curved lines on the sidecar.

3 Add an arm line on the passenger. Look at the motorcycle shapes emerging. Add these.

4 Look again! Starting at the top, draw the helmet and the driver.

5 Look at those happy faces. Add their faces. Draw other details you see.

6 Look at the final drawing. Erase extra sketch lines. Darken the final lines. Add color.

SUPER drawing! You are becoming a very talented cartoon artist!

Trike

Trikes are motorcycles with three tires instead of two. This will be the most complicated and challenging drawing you've done, so look closely at all of the details. You might want to use a ruler to get your straight lines just right.

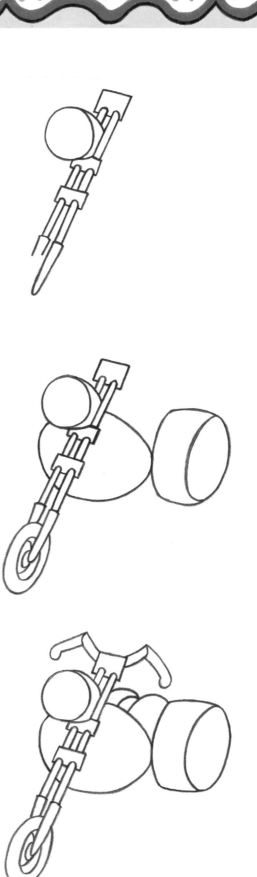

1 Look at the beginning lines and shapes. Sketch an oval for the headlight. Using curved and straight lines, draw the details of the steering fork.

2 Look again! Add a large gas tank behind the steering fork. Draw an oval and curved lines for the rear tire. Add the front tire.

3 Draw the curved handlebars. Using curved lines, add the seat and the top of a second back tire.

4 Look at the additional details. Starting at the top, add the details you see.

5 Look again! Add a cool cartoon face and any other details you see.

6 Look at the final drawing. Erase extra lines. Darken the final lines. Add color.

Magnificent job!
You are a great cartoonist!

Keep Going!

Now that you know how to draw cartoons, let you imagination run wild! Doodle away. Sketch freely, tweaking your drawing as you go along. As shapes begin to take form, turn them into a cartoon character!

Add little details just to see how they look. If you don't like them, you can always erase them. Go a little crazy. Add arms to trucks, shoes where tires would usually be, and anything wild that comes to mind. It's your drawing. Make it unique.

Just as exercising helps build big muscles, practicing your art will help you build strong drawing skills. This is the end of this book, but it's just the beginning for you to develop your own original cartoons!

Happy Cartooning!

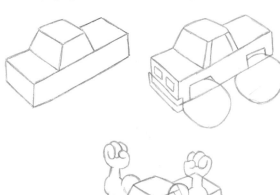

62

Award yourself! On the next page you'll find an award

certificate you can photocopy to let the world know you're

a **Cartoonist's Apprentice First Class!**

Have you enjoyed this book?

Find out about other books in this series
and see sample pages online at

www.123draw.com

Cartoonist's Apprentice First Class

THIS IS TO CERTIFY THAT

_____

HAS SUCCESSFULLY COMPLETED THE "1-2-3 DRAW CARTOON TRUCKS AND MOTORCYCLES" COURSE!

_____
DATE

Steve Barr
INSTRUCTOR

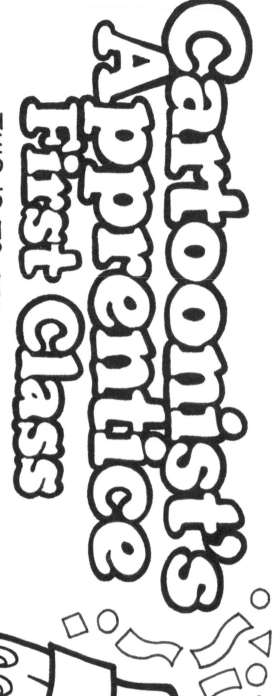